CW01467285

The BRF Book of 100 Prayers

15 The Chambers, Vineyard
Abingdon OX14 3FE
brf.org.uk

Bible Reading Fellowship is a charity (233280)
and company limited by guarantee (301324),
registered in England and Wales

ISBN 978 1 80039 147 5
First published 2022
10 9 8 7 6 5 4 3 2 1 0

Acknowledgements
Unless otherwise acknowledged, scripture quotations are taken from The Holy Bible, New International Version (Anglicised edition) copyright © 1979, 1984, 2011 by Biblica. Used by permission of Hodder & Stoughton Publishers, a Hachette UK company. All rights reserved. 'NIV' is a registered trademark of Biblica. UK trademark number 1448790.

Scripture quotation marked NCV taken from The Holy Bible, New Century Version®. Copyright © 2005 by Thomas Nelson, Inc. Scripture quotations marked NIRV are taken from the Holy Bible, New International Reader's Version®. Copyright © 1996, 1998 Biblica. All rights reserved throughout the world. Used by permission of Biblica. Scripture quotation marked KJV are taken from The Authorised Version of the Bible (The King James Bible), the rights in which are vested in the Crown, are reproduced by permission of the Crown's Patentee, Cambridge University Press. Scripture quotations marked NRSV are taken from The New Revised Standard Version of the Bible, Anglicised edition, copyright © 1989, 1995 by the Division of Christian Education of the National Council of the Churches of Christ in the United States of America. Used by permission. All rights reserved. Scripture quotation marked ESV is taken from The Holy Bible, English Standard Version, published by HarperCollins Publishers, © 2001 Crossway Bibles, a division of Good News Publishers. Used by permission. All rights reserved.

Every effort has been made to trace and contact copyright owners for material used in this resource. We apologise for any inadvertent omissions or errors, and would ask those concerned to contact us so that full acknowledgement can be made in the future.

A catalogue record for this book is available from the British Library

Printed and bound by CPI Group (UK) Ltd, Croydon CR0 4YY

The BRF *Book of* 100 *Prayers*

RESOURCING YOUR SPIRITUAL JOURNEY

Martyn Payne

Contents

Together through the generations

How should we live?

The BRF Centenary Prayer

Gracious God,
We rejoice in this centenary year
that you have grown BRF
from a local network of Bible readers
into a worldwide family of ministries.
Thank you for your faithfulness
in nurturing small beginnings
into surprising blessings.
We rejoice that, from the youngest to the oldest,
so many have encountered your word
and grown as disciples of Christ.
Keep us humble in your service,
ambitious for your glory
and open to new opportunities.
For your name's sake
Amen

Introduction

> **I cling to you; your right hand upholds me.**
> PSALM 63:8

One hundred years ago the western world was emerging from a pandemic known as Spanish flu. It has been estimated that up to 50 million people died; in fact, it's often forgotten that this represents many more deaths than occurred throughout the whole of the 1914–18 war, which had only come to an end four years previously. Almost everyone in the UK at that time could name a family member who had been killed in conflict or as a result of the contagion. And it was at such a time as this that the Bible Reading Fellowship was born in a church in Brixton in south London, attracting people to join Bible study and prayer groups supported by published daily notes. It was in such groups that people began to find faith and hope again in the God of peace who sent Jesus Christ to break down the dividing walls of hostility between us, offering to all a life beyond death that starts here and now.

That post-war and post-pandemic year of 1922 was a moment of opportunity that God used a century ago to give birth to an organisation that is still with us today. And one hundred years later, BRF is once again being used by God, in the wake of our own global pandemic, to resource and encourage churches and individuals 'to get a move on' spiritually – to borrow the words of BRF's founding father, Revd Leslie Mannering. The call to study the Bible as God's word and to deepen our life of prayer has never been more urgent now, as it was then.

Almost all the prayers collected in this book were written during the Covid-19 pandemic. They were inspired as a response to a crisis in a time of need, and indeed prayer often works like this. Of course, as Christians we know that regular times of prayer, whether extemporary or liturgical, are vital for healthy Christian discipleship. However, the truth is that we often forget to pray until a crisis comes and we are brought to our knees. While God does not cause the pain and the sadness that are part and parcel of life, he can use them to wake us up to what matters and bring us home to a safe place of love and grace.

The prayers in this book are a selection from a larger number that were posted on social media or published in the four-monthly BRF Prayer Diaries between March 2020 and the end of 2021 – throughout those Covid months whose long shadow is still with us. Although they come from that moment in time, they have also proved to be a prophetic and timeless source of comfort and inspiration to those who have used them. The positive feedback to these prayers has encouraged us to make them available in this centenary collection.

The book opens with a new prayer written for the BRF centenary. In a few short, memorable phrases, it offers us words to express our thankfulness and wonder at the way in which the Lord has used BRF to grow God's kingdom, both in this country and overseas, since 1922. BRF's publications, Bible reading notes and online resources, along with new ministries that encourage God's work among children, families, the elderly and those who are hearing the gospel for the first time, are all referenced in this prayer of celebration and praise.

For convenience of use, the one hundred new prayers that follow are divided into five sections, offering individuals and churches words to use in prayer:

- to help us come close to God
- to call out to God when we face the challenges of our Christian pilgrimage
- to praise God at festival times and on special occasions
- to support mission and ministry across the generations
- to use as we open up God's word and apply its truths to particular issues facing us today.

It is our hope that these prayers will be widely used, in both private and public worship. And finally, conscious that we often need encouragement to pray, we have included a selection of original thoughts on prayer throughout the book along with quotations from other Living Faith resources.

Prayer has always been at the heart of the movement of God's Spirit that has sustained the work of BRF over the past hundred years. None of our ministries, whether Anna Chaplaincy, Living Faith, Messy Church or Parenting for Faith, would be possible without the faithful support of those who pray for and with us. And so in recent years, we have nurtured a growing re-emphasis on this ministry of prayer. With this in mind, we hope that this collection will both enrich your own prayer life and help you to pray with us for all that God has in store for BRF in the future. And, adapting words from the centenary prayer, we pray that the prayers will encourage you 'to be ambitious for God's glory'.

Martyn Payne

Approaching God

Prayers of preparation
and thanksgiving

Come near to God and he will come near to you.
JAMES 4:8

1.

Thank you, Lord, for the gift of another day
in which you call us:
to bless our neighbour,
to welcome the stranger,
to pray for our enemies,
to look after your world,
to share the good news of your love,
and to become more like Jesus,
through the power of your Holy Spirit in us.
Amen

2.

Thank you for welcoming us
into your kingdom through the cross of Christ:
a kingdom where
the unforgivable are forgiven,
the undeserving rewarded,
the unlovable loved,
the wayward rescued,
the poor are rich,
the last are first
and the least are honoured,
because in each one of these
we can meet with you, Christ Jesus.
Amen

Christian prayer is... a face-to-face, heart-to-heart, Spirit-to-spirit connection with him who is the first and the last, the beginning and the end, the king of kings, and the lover of your soul.
LYNDALL BYWATER

Prayer isn't a silver bullet to solve our problems, nor a magic wand to make everything turn out well. It is our lifeline to God so that whatever happens we and God are in it together.
MARTYN PAYNE

3.

Gracious Father, as I settle myself to prayer,
your word reminds me that I am not alone,
but that I join the countless, invisible host of those
who are also praying to you at this time.

Loving Lord, as I settle myself to prayer,
your truth reminds me that it's not just me in this
place,
but that I join in the glorious worship of heaven
that never ceases,
and which surrounds my feeble words with a
chorus of praise.

Holy Spirit of God, as I settle myself to prayer,
your presence reminds me that it's not just this
moment,
but that I step into a place both in and beyond
time,
where all who have gone before and all who are
yet to come
sing of you, talk with you and rest in your love.
Amen

Prayer is not a words-based performance. Rather, it is the making of time and space for an authentic, personal and even intimate encounter with God the Father, who loves us and who 'knows what you need before you ask him'.

IAN ADAMS

4.

Every moment can be prayer – a time to listen to and receive from God.
Every place can contain parable – revealing and teaching God's ways.
Everything can be a taste of heaven – an opportunity to experience God's love.

So, am I always praying, wherever I am?
Am I always seeing new things about God, in whatever I encounter?
Am I always being changed into God's likeness, through whatever happens?

May prayer be the air I breathe.
May parables be the truths I see.
May preparation for heaven be the journey I walk.

As I receive from you in prayer, may you touch, bless and glorify all that is in my heart and mind.
As I meet with you in parable, may I learn to know you better through every experience every day.
As I trust you to equip me for heaven, may I be transformed and made ready for the beauty of eternity.
Amen

5.

I bend my knee, I bow my heart…
to reconnect with God and rekindle my desire
for him:
the source of all my being;
the end of all my becoming.

All things exist because of Christ
and all things hold together through him
and one day all things will be united in him.

Unless I dive afresh into the eternal river of the
Spirit of God each day,
I have no purpose, no power and no permanence
of my own;
I have no direction, no sustenance and no reason
to be.

For Jesus is my beginning, middle and my end:
and in him, I am made holy and made whole,
now and forever.
Amen

In Christ…
we are not just forgiven but heaven-bound;
we are not just blessed but safe forever;
we are not just loved for now but cherished for
eternity; knowing that Jesus is praying for us, with us,
in us, now, everywhere and always.
MARTYN PAYNE

6.

Lord, thank you that you are
all we need.
You give us forgiveness
for our inner well-being.
You give us sabbath
for our work-life balance.
You give us prayer
for our need of mindfulness.
You give us the example of Jesus
for our fulfilment.
You give us the power of the Spirit
for our lifestyle choices.
You give us the love of the Creator
for our motivation.
Lord, you are the door that leads to life.
Amen

7.

Dear Lord,
you invite us to pray.
Help us to know that,
when we don't know what to ask,
when we struggle to find the words,
when we become distracted and fall silent,
nevertheless our very desire to pray
for ourselves and others
is precious to you,
and is used to grow your kingdom
in ways beyond our imagining.
Amen

Before you start praying, take a moment to become aware of yourself and what's around you… Open your eyes, breathe deeply, let all your senses come alive and ask God to help you sense God's presence.
LYNDALL BYWATER

When you don't feel able to stand any more, try kneeling. It's the strongest place from which you can face the day.
MARTYN PAYNE

8.

We kneel before the mystery,
we bow beneath the glory,
we wait within the love,
we rest beside the presence,
we listen to the silence,
that we may receive in this moment,
more of the grace and the beauty of God in Christ.
Amen

Don't wait until you feel like praying.
Don't delay because you haven't got the words.
Don't stay silent because it is difficult.
Don't give up before you even try. 'Open your mouth,' says the Lord, 'and I will fill it.'
God is waiting to teach us how to pray.
MARTYN PAYNE

We need to make prayer part of our lives – indeed, a daily habit – if we want to learn to pray. Experts tell us that it takes the average person 30 days of doing the same thing before it becomes a habit.
JANE HOLLOWAY

Speak, Lord, for your servant is listening.
1 SAMUEL 3:10 (NCB)

9.

Listen!
The creator of the universe loves us!
What other devotion do we need?
'I have loved you with an everlasting love'
(Jeremiah 31:3).
The creator of the universe is on our side!
What other reassurance do we need?
'If God is for us, who can be against us?'
(Romans 8:31).
The creator of the universe sings our praise!
What other commendation do we need?
'You rejoice over us with singing' (Zephaniah
3:17).

Remember that the God who listens to you is the God who loves you. Whether God is saying yes or no… God is speaking to you in love… so ask God to tune your ears to the frequency of love.

LYNDALL BYWATER

10.

Lord, you have committed yourself
to love us to the end.
Help us to respond with
new depths to our loving,
new heights to our praising,
new lengths to our serving,
new breadths to our praying,
as we follow in the footsteps of Christ,
filled with your Holy Spirit.
Amen

The desire to pray can be fanned into flame by the presence of others around you who are praying. Just as faith is strengthened as we believe together, so prayer can reach new heights and depths when we pray alongside others.
MARTYN PAYNE

Learning how to be a Christian isn't about academic study in the way we usually understand it. It is fundamentally about prayer, from which the rest of life, including study, flows.
JOANNA COLLICUTT

11.

Word of the Father,
inspire our words this day,
speaking to us through the words we hear from others
and the words we read in our Bibles, daily notes and books
so that we might share words of encouragement with others.
Amen

Make friends with stillness; make friends with silence; make friends with solitude – these are some of the ways God will speak to us.
JANE HOLLOWAY

I don't know how the internet works! I don't understand so much of modern life, and yet I make use of it all and trust myself to it again and again. So why do I have any problem with miracles and the mystery of prayer?
MARTYN PAYNE

12.

Still our restless souls this day,
O Lord,
with the unshakeable awareness of your love
and the tangible certainty of your presence,
through Christ, our peace.
Amen

When you can't settle to pray; when the words won't come; when God seems silent or remote, know that your experience is not unique and hold onto the truth that it is then that the Spirit is praying for you with groans too deep for words.

MARTYN PAYNE

In Matthew 6:5–7, Jesus tells his disciples that the heart of prayer is to find a quiet space and use few words such as 'Love' and 'God'... If you keep a single word as a focus throughout the day, then this awareness goes with you... in all you do, through that one single sacred word.

DAVID COLE (BROTHER CASSIAN)

13.

God of glory, you are love.
We long to be
not just creatures in your image
but children in your family, who are:
love-shaped, love-filled,
love-empowered, love-multiplying,
just as you are.
Pour your love into our hearts
by your Holy Spirit.
In the name of Jesus,
Amen

When we pray, we're not telling or even asking God to do things; we are participating in a love relationship, and you don't need many words for that.
JOANNA COLLICUTT

Find your own special place, your own particular visuals, your own special style, your own way of praying to God. Prayer should be as unique and as individual as you yourself are.
MARTYN PAYNE

14.

Lord,
let me be the answer to someone's prayer today.
Lord,
help me to receive the answers to someone else's prayer for me today.
Lord,
use me as the answer to my own prayers today,
so I may encourage others with the stories of answered prayer every day.
Amen

The apostle Paul writes, 'All things are yes in Christ.' In other words, our prayers have already been answered, even before we pray them; and so our praying is all about us discovering and delighting in those answers.

MARTYN PAYNE

15.

Stir us up to serve you, Lord,
that in our serving, others may see you;
and, as others see you in us,
we may meet with you afresh in them,
so that we in turn are stirred again
to serve you with joy,
day after day.
Amen

Our God is fully committed this day
to helping us do our best
with who we are
with what we have
with where we have been
and with where we are going
through the Holy Spirit in us.
MARTYN PAYNE

Prayer can be seen as something of an unfolding adventure. Our understanding of prayer deepens over time and reflects a growing intimacy with God.
TONY HORSFALL

16.

Lord Jesus,
who came to give us life in all its fullness,
draw us daily closer to you,
so that we might come closer
to the beauties of your creation
to the gift of one another
and to the wonder of the Father's love.
Amen

No rhythm of prayer is ever complete when it only concerns us and our issues. We are given the gift of prayer that we might use it to unleash blessing on the world around us. And each of us has a circle of people and situations we get to bless – family, friends, neighbours, work colleagues.

LYNDALL BYWATER

A fawning etiquette of unctuous prayer is actually foreign to the Bible. Biblical prayer is impertinent, persistent, shameless and indecorous. It is more like haggling in an outdoor bazaar than the polite monologues of the church.

WALTER WINK

17.

Open our eyes, gracious Lord, to see
the infinite value of every soul,
the supreme importance of every human life
and the unique beauty of every individual
so that, without distraction or agenda,
we might catch a glimpse
of your likeness mirrored and your love at work
in each person with whom
we spend time this day.
Amen

We express our trust in God, and we put our hope in him, through prayer. The practice of prayer assures us in faith that if we're waiting on God, then we won't miss out on anything.

MARK BRADFORD

18.

Loving Father,
may all our experiences, conversations
  and thoughts
be seasoned with salt,
be full of grace,
be alive with hope,
so that the things of this earth
might begin to taste of heaven,
through Christ our Lord.
Amen

Just as gravity connects us to earth, so prayer draws us to heaven, so that we may live safely in the balanced space between the two, where the Father, the Son and the Spirit are pleased to find a home.
MARTYN PAYNE

Prayer is the place where our perspective broadens and our understanding deepens. It's the place where God's Spirit shows us what we need to see.
LYNDALL BYWATER

19.

Lord, you are love
and in you is no unlove at all.
May your love be at work in us this day,
so we might be all love too.
We thank you
for all the love we have witnessed,
for all the love we have received,
and for all the love you've enabled us to share,
because without love we are nothing.
Amen

Prayer is a conversation of love that is already going on within the Trinity and includes everything we mean by prayer – intimacy, adoration, love, concern for the world. Our prayer… is about joining in that conversation.

ANN PERSSON

Prayer doesn't have to be complicated, wordy, clever or even beautiful. In fact, it is just our soul crying out for help or responding with thanks to whatever life puts in our path.

MARTYN PAYNE

20.

Holy Spirit of God,
stir up in us your fruit of goodness
that, like Jesus,
we may go about doing good
whenever we can
and for whomever we meet this day,
for the sake of the kingdom of God.
Amen

In prayer we remind ourselves of the Father who created us; of the Lord Jesus whose love holds us safe and of the Holy Spirit who works creatively in and through us. This is how each day's discipleship starts.
MARTYN PAYNE

It is because God loves us that he knows what we need... If only we could relax into the fact that God's relationship with us is absolutely secure, we would find that we don't need so many words.
JOANNA COLLICUTT

Prayers for the journey

In times of change and hardship

No matter what happens, tell God about everything. Ask and pray, and give thanks to him. Then God's peace will watch over your hearts and your minds.

PHILIPPIANS 4:6–7 (NIRV)

21.

Lord Jesus,
you invite us to entrust
our troubled hearts into your safekeeping,
our restless spirits into your loving care,
our puzzled minds into your stilling presence.
As we do so,
may we find our way home
into the reality of the living God
through your cross and resurrection,
which is our only hope.
Amen

When we decide to turn to God in thanksgiving, when we determine to trust and not be afraid, as he has again and again invited us to do, something of God's nature is made real in us.

JOANNA COLLICUTT

Intercessory prayer isn't simply about obtaining particular answers, but about those we pray for coming ever closer to God's love and presence. Prayer is about being faithful, being open, being attentive and waiting on God's timing.

MARTYN PAYNE

22.

Lord,
it's hard to look beyond what we can see.
Open our eyes of faith to know
that there is more,
that there is better,
that there is greater,
and that there is heaven all around.
And in the light of this bigger vision
to see what we do see differently.
Amen

As we pray, we lift our eyes beyond the 'now' of our own struggles and the griefs of those for whom we pray, to catch a glimpse of the bigger picture and the long view, which is God's eternal perspective.
MARTYN PAYNE

23.

Where are you, Lord?

In the voice on the phone; in the smile
across the street;
in the kindness of strangers; in the courage of
carers;
in the laughter online; in the colours of spring;
in the stories of hope; in the instinct to pray;
in the wisdom of people; in the words of the book.
Child, here I am.

The psalmist writes, 'The sound of God's voice has gone out in all the universe.' In other words, Radio God is always and everywhere on air. Prayer starts by tuning into that sound.
MARTYN PAYNE

We pray because God himself modelled in Jesus the life of prayer. Jesus did not say 'if you pray' but 'when you pray'.
JANE HOLLOWAY

Prayer helps us to have the strength to deal with what we will face when we get up from our knees.
TIMOTHY BAVIN OSB

24.

Never-failing God,
keep us when we grow weary,
cheer us when we become despondent,
hold us when we lose heart,
and help us to keep looking to Jesus,
the pioneer and perfecter of our faith.
Amen

Lord, take me where you want me to go; let me meet who you want me to meet; tell me what you want me to say; and keep me out of your way.

FATHER MYCHAL JUDGE

Pray as you can; pray as you are; pray as you feel. Don't try and imitate others or be intimidated into praying like someone else. It is you God wants to meet when you pray.

MARTYN PAYNE

25.

Loving God,
when our everyday lives seem too much to bear,
and our personal circumstances threaten to
overwhelm us,
reach out your hand to rescue us
and set us on the solid ground of your love
once again.
Amen

By punctuating the day with specific intentional stops for prayer, it is easier to engage with the struggles and joys of life. This doesn't stop us praying at any other time, but it does ensure that prayer flows through our whole day.
DAVID COLE (BROTHER CASSIAN)

26.

Lord Jesus,
you promised to be with us to the end of time.
Please be with us
when we reach the end of our tether,
the end of our strength,
the end of our patience,
and bring us safely through to you,
the end of all our longing.
Amen

Whatever we are experiencing,
God is with us;
Wherever we go, God is close beside us;
However we feel, God is moved within us;
And when death comes, God will offer Jesus
on our behalf.
God is our forever, and for all things,
God of love.

MARTYN PAYNE

27.

Thank you, Father that…
whatever we experience, you are here with us,
wherever we go, you are close beside us,
however we feel, you are moved within us,
and whenever death comes,
you are ready to welcome us through Christ.
Thank you that you are our forever and for
all things,
God of love.
Amen

Make sure that your daily time of reflection and prayer, study and reading, begins and ends in praise. Spend time thanking God for his act of creation, sing songs or read passages from the psalms out loud to remind yourself of God's goodness.

SALLY WELCH

Faith is believing that our prayers are heard. The truth that God who loves us hears every prayer is itself an answer to our prayers and possibly the best answer we need.

MARTYN PAYNE

28.

Lord, who travelled
from heaven to earth and back again
for our sake,
sustain us as we journey in faith
on unknown paths;
trusting that you are
both alongside us
and also ahead of us,
ready to welcome us home
at our destination with joy.
Amen

Prayer is at its heart reminding ourselves every single day that God made us, God loves us and God is with us. Everything else flows from these eternal truths.
MARTYN PAYNE

Whether or not it comes naturally to you, a rhythm of prayer will always need to include the practice of stillness. As you make space to stop, so you settle yourself in a place where the Light can reach you.
LYNDALL BYWATER

29.

Father God,
when the news is bleak, steady us;
when the pain is bitter, surround us;
when the days blur, sustain us;
when despair burdens, still us.
In our weakness, make us strong;
in our lowness, lift us up,
confident that our Redeemer
ever lives and prays for us
and will never let us go.
Amen

When we take seriously the many ills of our world, from climate change to the cries of the displaced and the suffering, it can be overwhelming. But then we remember that 'with God all things are possible' and we pray.

MARTYN PAYNE

'Life has its rhythms,' David Adam says. 'We all need to be able to cope with its ebb and flow. We have to survive its darkness as well as its light; to survive this intricate pattern, we need to have an overriding rhythm of prayer.'

DAVID COLE (BROTHER CASSIAN)

30.

Teach us, O Lord,
what is important about life.
May we not squander it on self;
may we not spoil it with sin;
may we not spend it on the surface,
but live it by grace and with gratitude
for your glory.
Amen

Prayer is one of God's greatest gifts to us – the ability to communicate directly with the Almighty. Prayer is the first sign of new life.
TONY HORSFALL

31.

Loving God,
who in Christ stepped into the mess of our world,
and who, on the cross, was messed up for us,
we bring before you our messy lives.
Forgive us, and by your Spirit at work in us,
help us to step out in love and faith
to bring healing to this messy world.
Amen

'Lord Jesus Christ, son of God, have mercy on me, a sinner' – this simple prayer is not so much about our sins or a status as sinners, but a humble, continual prayer of reorientation towards the God who loves us.

IAN ADAMS

'Thank you. Help. Heal. Wow! Where are you? What next? I'm sorry.' These are the foundation stones of prayer.

MARTYN PAYNE

32.

Gracious God,
thank you for choosing us as your disciples
and calling us to serve you in this world.
Help us to work out this calling in every season
and circumstance,
through change, challenges and times of
uncertainty,
trusting that, having begun this good work in us,
you will bring it to completion on the day of
Christ.
In his name,
Amen

Prayer is about God changing us. It isn't primarily about getting what we asked for but always about staying close to God. It isn't primarily about asking, but listening and therefore discovering what God wants us to be, to become and to do.
MARTYN PAYNE

Praying 'in the name of Jesus' means to pray 'in accordance with his nature', and this is the essence of the Christian life.
JOANNA COLLICUTT

33.

God of our life's pilgrimage,
we know that in company with you,
no experience is wasted,
no encounter is by chance,
no episode on our journey is without meaning.
Help us to go on bearing fruit into old age,
until you call us home.
Amen

Here am I. Send me!
ISAIAH 6:8

34.

Keeper of our steps,
keeper of our senses,
keeper of our souls,
keep us as the apple of your eye;
keep us in your perfect peace;
keep us in our going out and our coming in;
for you are the strong Keep
within the walls of our life.
Amen

Prayer is the place where we draw nourishment from God. We bring our needs and we draw on his provision; we bring our failures and we draw on his grace; we bring our brokenness and we draw on his healing.
LYNDALL BYWATER

Learn to tune into God's prayer-waves each day. The more we do this, the better the reception we experience.
MARTYN PAYNE

35.

Life-giving,
love-bringing,
home-making God,
may the shelter of your presence
bring hope and healing
to all those who have been
uprooted and stranded in unfamiliar lands
because of the brokenness of this world.
Amen

My child, hear my voice
through the unexpected thoughts in your head,
through the surprise words of strangers,
through the 'annoying' interruptions of your day,
through the persistent instincts that prompt you from deep within,
and through words spoken to others, recorded in scripture, in song and in inspirational writing.

MARTYN PAYNE

36.

Long-suffering, promise-keeping God,
you always act at the right time,
because your purposes are rooted in eternity;
grant us a faith that can wait
and a patience that can trust
in your big-picture plans
for the detail of our lives.
Through Christ,
whose coming and saving was prepared
before the world began,
Amen

Prayer changes us as we wait and hope. We become more aware of the needs of others, more aware of the presence of God, more aware of God, even in the silence of unanswered prayer.
SALLY WELCH

All life becomes prayer in as much as we learn to set aside special moments and places for regular prayer. The one creates and shapes the other, in the same way as whole-life worship grows out of times of gathered worship.
MARTYN PAYNE

37.

Lord,
when you tell me not to worry,
please also remind me of your promises.

Lord,
when you tell me not to fear,
please also remind me of your presence.

Lord,
when you tell me not to give up,
please also remind me of your power.

For you, Lord, are not only the Christ who leads us
but also the Spirit who inspires us
on our life's journey with you.
Amen

Spirit of God, turn my raw feelings into passionate prayers.
MICHAEL MITTON

Have you ever felt like your words in prayer are useless? That they are just falling to the floor when they leave your mouth or hitting the ceiling instead of penetrating heaven? Perhaps that is because God is wanting you to stop using words and be drawn into the deeper way of silence.
DAVID COLE

38.

God of all comfort,
strengthener within
inspirer beyond
and supporter alongside,
you uphold us in mind, body and spirit
with your wrap-around care.
Help us in our turn
to pass on that sure and certain comfort to others
in the name of Christ our Lord.
Amen

Desperation, need, pain and fear are unavoidable aspects of our lives on earth. God's plan isn't always to take these away but to turn them into springboards to prayer.

MARTYN PAYNE

39.

Lord of all life and love,
walk with us throughout our pilgrimage on earth,
teaching us daily
how to bless others through service,
how to find strength in weakness,
and how to experience growth by letting go,
for your name's sake.
Amen

Changing things through prayer can take a long time and is hard work. Jesus needs people who will keep on praying and never give up… remembering that God's ways are higher than our ways… and Jesus-people call this 'mystery'.
LUCY MOORE

Just as we know that there are sound frequencies outside the range of the human ear, in the same way the voice of God seems to be silent but in truth is always present.
MARTYN PAYNE

40.

Creator God,
by whose Spirit we exist
so that we might bear fruit for you,
may we measure our lives this day
not by what we achieve or possess,
but by how much we give,
how many we love
and how often we hear
your 'well done, good and faithful servant'.
Amen

P R A Y: Pause In the presence of God… Reflect on the love of God… Accept the forgiveness of God because of Jesus… and say Yes to the power of God at work in us this day.

MARTYN PAYNE

A simple prayer gets God's attention more quickly than any long psalm mumbled mindlessly through closed teeth. That's why the Christian tradition says that 'a short prayer penetrates heaven'.

DAVID COLE (BROTHER CASSIAN)

Seasons of the Christian year

Seek the Lord and the strength he gives.

PSALM 105:4 (NIRV)

Harvest

41.

Hope-giving God,
thank you for creating a world full of seeds
that testify to your loving investment
in the land and in our lives.
Just as you rejoice to see those seeds bear fruit,
we come to you at this festival time
with the fruit of praise and thanksgiving
for your goodness and faithful love.
Amen

In prayer we bow before:
The love that can't stop loving.
The gift that can't stop giving.
The light that can't stop enlightening.
The blessing that can't stop blessing.
We kneel before our God who never changes.
MARTYN PAYNE

I am pleased that you teach sacred theology to the brothers, providing that… you do not extinguish the spirit of prayer and devotion during study of this kind.
ST FRANCIS OF ASSISI

42.

Lord, as tenants of your kingdom,
you have committed to us
the harvesting of our fields and of our faith.
Forgive us for the failed harvests that are our responsibility,
and help us to respond better to your cultivation and care
by bringing forth the fruits of faith, hope and love,
that alone can transform this world and bring joy in heaven.
Amen

As we turn in prayer to God, the great Creator, we become vessels of creative energy and desire. We long to give expression to the gift we have received, and as we do so, the act of creation becomes a prayer in itself.
DANIEL WOLPERT

43.

Father God,
because there is always enough
and more with you
teach us to trust in your plenty,
so that we give what we can
and share what we have,
daring to leave the overflow of your harvest to us
for others to glean.
Amen

Work and prayer are opposite sides of the great coin of a life that is both holy and useful, immersed in God.
JOAN CHITTISTER

Closely structured prayer proves to be the platform from which spontaneous prayer bursts. I have learnt to value both elements.
GEORGE LINGS

Waiting in prayer is a disciplined refusal to act before God acts.
EUGENE PETERSON

Remembrance

44.

Remembering God,
you never forget to keep promises and show
mercy,
and through Christ you re-member us in love.
Thank you that the death of those dear to us
matters to you.
Just as Jesus promised the dying thief
that he would be remembered in heaven,
so we can be sure that they will be remembered
because your memory never fails;
and whether we live or whether we die
we and they will be with you forever.
Amen

Entering into the place of prayer: the faithfulness of the Son opens up the door. The foreverness of the Father has already prepared the room. The fullness of the Spirit floods this space with light.

MARTYN PAYNE

45.

Eternal God,
even though we live in the shadow of death,
which takes from us those we love,
through war, disease, old age and accident,
nevertheless you have shown us in Christ
that your love is stronger than death.
Please sustain us with this truth
and comfort us with your gift of life
that can never die.
Amen

Lord, to whom shall we go? You have the words of eternal life.
JOHN 6:68

46.

God of resurrection and hope,
as once again the last post sounds
on this Remembrance Day.
and we name all those who have died before
their time
in wars and pandemics,
help us also to look forward to the sound of the
last trumpet
that will awake the dead,
and will welcome us and them into everlasting
life.
Through Christ our Lord,
Amen

To be an intercessor is to be a go-between. Intercession is bringing people and situations to God, bringing God to people and situations, and doing all of it through prayer.
LYNDALL BYWATER

When you can't settle to pray; when the words won't come; when God seems silent or remote, know that your experience is not unique and hold onto the truth that it is then that the Spirit is praying for you with groans too deep for words.
MARTYN PAYNE

Advent

47.

God of prophecy,
speak into our Advent waiting
with words of inspiration and courage,
that we might find in you
a great light in our darkness,
a voice in our wilderness,
a highway in our desert,
and a new bloom in our dry land.
We wait for you, we look to you,
desire of all the nations,
and hope of the whole world.
Amen

Praying draws us into an ever-greater awareness of God's presence beyond, beside, among and within us.
MARTYN PAYNE

48.

Mighty God,
who chose to come to us
not in a consuming fire, nor a destructive
earthquake,
but with the unexpected cry of a baby.
Meet us with mercy and grace;
mould us afresh as a people of faith;
make us new with your healing presence;
because you are a God who forgives
and works for those who wait for you.
Come, our Lord and our God, come.
Amen

Prayer is a mystery, but that doesn't mean it's beyond us. Let the good habit of wanting to pray and trying to pray regularly carry you through to an experience of prayer that is ever richer and deeper.
MARTYN PAYNE

This practice of the Presence of God is somewhat hard at the outset, yet [it] leads the soul insensibly to the ever-present vision of God… which is the most spiritual and real, the most free and most life-giving manner of prayer.
BROTHER LAWRENCE

49.

It's time to get ready,
it's time to remember,
it's time to rehearse the great story,
it's time to celebrate your coming
both into our world and into our lives.
May the truth, the wonder and the power of
this time
touch us ever more deeply this Advent.
Amen

Prayer is... the simplest and most complex thing I know. At its simplest, it's us talking with God. But it's also the story of human beings communicating with one who exists outside of time and eternity.
LYNDALL BYWATER

Some people say, 'I'm sending you good vibes,' or maybe, 'I'm wishing you well.' They might not know it but what motivates them is our God-given desire to pray. God wove this instinct into our DNA from the very beginning.
MARTYN PAYNE

50.

Advent Lord,
like sentinels on the city walls,
we watch;
like servants at the master's table,
we wait;
like search parties through the long night
we are awake;
for the dawn of your coming,
for the morning star to rise in our hearts,
and for the renewal of our salvation.
Amen

We do not know what to do, but our eyes are on you.
2 CHRONICLES 20:12

Christmas

51.

The patriarchs were promised it.
The prophets foretold it.
The people longed for it.
The nations sought it.
And now in our time, it has come.
Salvation is here!
It has dawned on us from on high.
Thank you, Father, for Jesus.
Amen

I pray because I can't help myself. I pray because I'm helpless. I pray because the need flows out of me all the time, waking and sleeping. It doesn't change God. It changes me.

C.S. LEWIS

Prayer happens when the things of earth and the things of heaven agree, and because of Christ that agreement is already guaranteed on God's side, so it is now over to us to respond.

MARTYN PAYNE

New Year

52.

God of new beginnings,
God of a new heaven and a new earth,
God of new creations,
God of yesterday, today and forever,
we come to you to start again.
There is no better place to be.
Amen

We can learn best how to pray by trying to pray. It takes just one or two notes from us and the Holy Spirit will supply the backing track, even a whole orchestra to carry our little tune to God.
MARTYN PAYNE

Philippians 4:13 is known as the 'ten-finger prayer', as each word corresponds to the fingers of both hands. Instead of counting to ten in times of anger or stress, try taking a deep breath and counting off this 'prayer' on your fingers, one by one.
SALLY WELCH

Lent

53.

Creator God and Saviour,
who chose in love to make this world,
inviting us to share in its care, renewal
    and nurture,
forgive us for the many wrong choices we
    have made.
This Lent, we choose again to join with you
in the reconciling and healing of all things,
as by your Spirit you both renew the face
    of the earth
and also restore us in your image
through the death and resurrection of
    Jesus Christ our Lord.
Amen

There's an old saying that goes like this: seven prayerless days make one weak. The truth is that even one prayerless day leaves us vulnerable.

MARTYN PAYNE

Holy Week

54.

Suffering Lord,
just as you chose on the cross
to share our pain and embrace our dying,
may we accompany those we care for
  at the end of their days,
with the assurance of
separation ending
shadows scattering
and a more glorious story beginning
through your resurrection love.
Amen

My strength is made perfect in weakness...
when I am weak, then am I strong.
2 CORINTHIANS 12:9–10 (KJV)

55.

Holy and pain-bearing God,
who on the cross
experienced desolation and despair,
walk with us through this present darkness
and grant us a glimpse of your glory to come.
Amen

God may answer our prayers with: 'Yes, I thought you'd never ask!'; 'Yes, but not yet'; 'Yes, but not in the way that you think': or sometimes with, 'No, because I love you too much.'
PETE GREIG

Crying out that you simply have no words to pray is itself of course a prayer. An honest shouting into the darkness is in fact calling on the name of the Lord without realising it.
MARTYN PAYNE

Easter

56.

Death-defeating,
darkness-chasing,
door-opening God,
may the truth of the resurrection
light up our world this day,
helping us to live differently,
love fearlessly
and lean faithfully on Jesus
for whatever lies ahead.
Amen

Jesus prayed for his friends and for those who would believe in him through their witness. Jesus continues to pray for us now in heaven. And Jesus's prayers were answered even though the answer was the defeat of the cross before the victory of the resurrection.
MARTYN PAYNE

There is no labour greater than that of prayer to God… Prayer is warfare to the last breath.
ABBA AGATHON

57.

On the first day of Creation,
God said, 'Let there be light!'
On the first day of Resurrection,
the Father said, 'Let there be Jesus!'
Rejoice therefore that the darkness is passing,
as the dayspring from on high dawns upon us.
Halleluiah!

We spend time with God because in Christ
God spent all for us.
MARTYN PAYNE

58.

Jesus walks with us in our sorrows,
unrecognised.
Christ touches us in our confusion,
unexpected.
Jesus burns within us in our longing,
unseen.
Christ sits with us in our loneliness,
unknown.
Jesus eats with us in our home,
untroubled.
Christ reveals through his hands and side,
sin undone and love unimaginable.
Christ Jesus keeps us on life's journeys,
under the shelter of his love.
Amen

Christian prayer means starting small. If you ever feel you're not sophisticated enough, theological enough, articulate enough, holy enough to pray, then you are exactly in the right frame of mind for an encounter with God.

LYNDALL BYWATER

Ascension Day

59.

Lord Jesus Christ,
ascended to heaven
reigning in heaven,
and praying from heaven on our behalf,
clothe us with power from on high
as you fill us with your Holy Spirit,
so that,
just as you took earth into heaven,
we might bring heaven to earth,
in your name.
Amen

Prayer requires us to be attentive and to turn our attention in the right direction… we must lay aside too many words, be prepared to turn our hearts upwards and seek a heavenly perspective.
JOANNA COLLICUTT

Our prayer is God's bridgehead into the lives of all for whom we pray.
MARTYN PAYNE

Pentecost

60.

Holy Spirit of God,
as you come alongside
to convict, counsel and comfort us,
bring to mind your words to us,
pour into our hearts your love toward us,
fill our lives with your gifts to share with others
and be a never-failing presence within us,
on our journey through life
for your name's sake.
Amen

Prayer should be short and pure, unless perhaps it is prolonged under the inspiration of divine grace. In community, however, prayer should always be brief.
THE RULE OF ST BENEDICT

Together through the generations

Praise God, young men and women.
Praise God, old men and children.
Let them praise the name of the Lord,
for his name alone is exalted;
his splendour is above the earth
and the heavens.

PSALM 148:12–13

61.

The Anna Chaplaincy prayer

Faithful God,
you have promised in Christ to be with us
to the end of time.
Come close to those who have lived long and
experienced much.
Help them to continue to be faithful and,
within the all-age kingdom of God,
to find ways to go on giving and receiving
your grace, day by day.
For your glory and your kingdom.
Amen

As we pray, we invite God's presence and power to touch the lives of others.
MARTYN PAYNE

62.

The Messy Church prayer

Holy Spirit of God,
whose energy and gifts equip us to share the
good news of Jesus,
strengthen local Messy Church teams as they
plan their services,
granting them ideas for activities,
inspiration for celebrations
and grace for the welcome and the meal,
so that adults and children might be drawn
into a community of faith, hope and love,
centred on Christ.
Amen

Prayer is so simple that a child can do it. And yet so profound that the greatest theologians cannot fully comprehend how it works.

TONY HORSFALL

Maybe we should stop over-worrying about how we should pray to God and instead remember that God is always praying for us. And God is praying for our best – that's what God's blessing means.

MARTYN PAYNE

63.

The Parenting for Faith prayer

Loving God,
you created us to know you and be known by you
in a safe relationship of love.
Help all who are parents, godparents,
grandparents and guardians
to pray for the children in their care,
to model lives of faith,
and to encourage an experience of God-
connectedness for their journey through life.
In the name of Jesus,
Amen

Prayer is not just a relationship with God; it is also a powerful weapon, which we have been given to use wisely as we work to bring in God's kingdom.
JANE HOLLOWAY

Our priestly calling in prayer is to turn up before God 'wearing the ephod' on which are named all those 'from our tribe' whom God has put on our heart.
MARTYN PAYNE

64.

The Living Faith prayer

Word of God,
help us to speak and to write
words of encouragement for each other;
and help us to hear and to read
words of inspiration from each other;
drawing on the Bible notes we study,
the Christian books on which we reflect,
and the Bible truths we explore,
so that each of these words
might shape and direct our lives to your glory.
Amen

[Let me] encourage you to experiment with different prayer postures (kneeling, lying face down or face up, standing, arms raised, head bowed and so on). Prayer postures can be an aid in helping us move from head to heart as we come before God. Also this way, you may be able to communicate to God what your words fail to convey.

LARRY WARNER

65.

A discipleship prayer

Covenant God,
you promise to bring to fulfilment
the gift of faith you have sown in our lives.
Prompt us daily
to get a move on spiritually
and to keep our eyes on Jesus,
throughout our lifelong journey of following you.
Amen

Pray as you can, not as you can't.
Pray as you are, not as someone else.
Pray as you feel, not pretending otherwise.
Pray whenever, wherever, however often you want,
because God is always waiting to talk with you.
MARTYN PAYNE

Prayers for the generations working together

66.

Timeless God,
you long for blessings to overflow
from one generation to another
as the young strengthen the old
and the old inspire the young.
Teach us how to honour every age group
and every section of our community,
so that none is left behind
and none is left out
in the ageless kingdom of heaven.
Amen

To be a Christian without prayer is no more possible than to be alive without breathing.
MARTIN LUTHER

67.

God of the youngest and the oldest,
you rejoice in the first smile of a child
and the last song of a grandparent.
May each generation be blessed
by meeting with you in the other,
and by representing you to each other,
in the all-age kingdom of God.
Amen

Prayer is never about persuading God, but it is sometimes about partnering with him in seeing a difficult situation resolved.
LYNDALL BYWATER

Our prayers always get through to God… we never get the 'engaged' or 'number unobtainable' tones. We will never be put on hold 'because all our lines are busy'!
JANE HOLLOWAY

68.

Gracious God,
you are older than time and yet your mercies
are new every morning.
Help us to rediscover the gifts that the elderly
can bring to the young
and the young to the elderly, both in church
and in our communities,
so that we might bless and encourage each other
to grow in our Christian discipleship.
Through Jesus Christ our Lord,
Amen

Through prayer we open ourselves to change: we are the ones who come to see something different about others, experience something new in our situation or are given fresh insights into our circumstances. This is primarily how God works in answer to prayer.
MARTYN PAYNE

Let us aspire to prayerful work: we can both do God's work when we pray and also pray while we work, making our work holy. Our work this day can be our prayer and the glory that we give to God.
GORDON GILES

69.

Almighty God,
Father, Son and Holy Spirit,
you are love in community: three in one and one in three.
Draw us away from our narrow individualism to a new understanding of togetherness
where differences are welcomed and celebrated
and where all ages and experiences can work together to bring in your kingdom on earth.
For your glory and in your name,
Amen

Prayer is born out of our need to be helped; is refined in the fire of our being helpless; and is matured in the experience of our being held.
MARTYN PAYNE

70.

God of all people,
children and grandparents,
teenagers and elderly,
young adults and godparents,
the working and retired,
the single and married,
help us all to honour and celebrate each other,
in communities of grace and love
for your glory.
Amen

Seek to enter each prayer experience this week, expectation-free and desiring simply to 'show up', presenting yourself as a living sacrifice, 'holy and pleasing to God – which is your true and proper worship' (Romans 12:1).
LARRY WARNER

71.

Dear God,
who created all people in your image,
teach us to value each other across the
generations,
and to listen and learn from each other's stories,
knowing that in meeting another,
we are always on holy ground.
Amen

Embracing prayer as a way of life means being sensitive to people's needs and immediately taking them to God in prayer, asking for guidance and strength in any action we take.
IAN ADAMS

It's God's Spirit who prompts us to pray, because God's love is longing to bless, through God's Son who has made it possible.
MARTYN PAYNE

72.

God who promises to bless us,
our children and our children's children,
teach us to honour every generation
so that none is left out or left behind
in the ageless kingdom of heaven.
Amen

At different times in our lives, using a variety of ways of praying can help us not to give up. Whether it is extempore prayer, set prayer, silent prayer or corporate prayer, find the way to pray that suits you right now, in your present circumstances.

MARTYN PAYNE

If there is anywhere on earth, a lover of God who is always kept safe, I know nothing of it, for it was not shown to me. But this was shown: that in falling and rising again we are always kept in that same precious love.

JULIAN OF NORWICH

73.

Giving thanks for Messy Church values of Christ-centredness, all-age, creativity, hospitality and celebration

Thank you that we serve and share
a hug-offering,
a play-delighting,
a community-building,
a sin-forgiving,
a party-throwing,
God of love.
Amen

It's amazing how hung up we still get on words when we pray. God who communicates through nature and music, children's laughter and a friend's touch, doesn't need us to stick to words when we talk with him.

LYNDALL BYWATER

Even the simple act of naming another person before God is prayer.

MARTYN PAYNE

74.

A prayer for those who do not yet know your name

Spirit of Jesus,
you long to open the eyes of all
to the experience of God's love.
Stir up in our friends and neighbours
a hunger for the meaning of life
that is found by coming home to you;
and stir us to play our part
in sharing your love in word and deed.
Amen

Prayers for parents and our homes

75.

Dear God, our perfect parent,
you call us to pass on the story of your faithfulness
to our children and our children's children.
Help us to parent, godparent and grandparent
the next generations
through prayer and by our example.
For your kingdom's sake,
Amen

The poet Tennyson wrote, 'More things are wrought by prayer than this world dreams of.' Our prayers are the indispensable building material for the kingdom of God on earth.

MARTYN PAYNE

The astonishing privilege of prayer is that it is the means by which we connect with God's heart, and, as we do so, our own hearts start to line up with God's.

LYNDALL BYWATER

76.

Loving God, come close to Christian parents in
our congregations.
As they seek to nurture faith in their children,
may they be blessed by the faith of those in their
care,
so that together they can create 'little churches'
at home
through the presence of your Holy Spirit.
Amen

We need the transforming power of the gospel to shape and renew us. That is why a regular pattern for prayer and Bible reading is so helpful. It becomes the foundation upon which a Christian life is built.
STEPHEN COTTRELL

Don't over-spiritualise prayer. It is not some holy superpower or some high-level spiritual attribute for the few. Praying is to our spirits what breathing is to our bodies. It is what Christians do while they negotiate life.
MARTYN PAYNE

Prayers for older people

77.

Lord of time and eternity,
who never cease to walk alongside us on our life's journey,
assure those facing old age of your continuing presence.
Comfort them when they face bereavement, limitations or illness
and grant them and those who care for them each day
a rich experience of your grace at work in their lives.
In Jesus' name,
Amen

I lift up my eyes to the hills – from where will my help come? My help comes from the Lord, who made heaven and earth.
PSALM 121:1–2 (NRSV)

78.

O God of the weakest and the most vulnerable,
walk beside those in the last years of their lives.
Keep them safe,
as they lose control,
become more dependent,
and need to be held by those charged with
their care,
during the final stages of their journey home
to heaven.
Amen

As we develop our 'prayer muscles', we have the example before us of the greatest athlete of all, Christ himself, who is not only the goal of the race, but is also our running companion; while all the time, the race is being run in the company of a crowd of supporters cheering us on.

SALLY WELCH

Prayers for our schools

79.

Dear Lord of all our questions and answers,
who opened minds through parables
and touched lives with healing compassion,
help all those who are called to teach,
granting them creative ideas for learning,
and sensitive hearts to the needs of each child
in their care.
Amen

Christian prayer always has an exit sign: we step out of life, we go in to encounter the living God and then he sends us back out into the world. If you never want to be given a job to do, a mountain to climb or a person to care for, then avoid Christian prayer at all costs.
LYNDALL BYWATER

80.

Dear God,
thank you for our schools with their teachers
and children.
Together may they create:
safe places for young lives to flourish,
happy places for wonder and discovery,
hopeful places of peace and healing,
stimulating places of learning and laughter,
and places where old and young can find purpose
and direction in life.
Amen

Christian prayer is the language of those who choose to live for God in the company of Jesus, whatever is happening in their lives and wherever they find themselves.
MARTYN PAYNE

How should we live?

I want you to pray for all people. Ask God
to help and bless them. Give thanks for them…
Pray that we can live peaceful and quiet lives.
And pray that we will be godly and holy.

1 TIMOTHY 2:1–2 (NIRV)

Prayers on the theme of creation care

81.

Gracious God,
you have planned in Christ to restore all things:
our relationship with you,
our love for one another,
our care for your world,
and our concern for every living creature
under heaven.
Help us to embrace this high calling as
your people
and to be committed to
planet-care and people-justice
as much as personal salvation.
For your name's sake,
Amen

We come closer to our best self when we are not the centre of our own lives. Praise, prayer and service of others are God's gifts to us that help that happen.
MARTYN PAYNE

82.

Creator God,
who once looked at what you had made
and pronounced it 'good',
forgive us for damaging this goodness
with greed, selfishness and neglect.
May your grace poured out to us in Christ Jesus
transform both our attitude to one another
and towards this world you have given us,
so that as caretakers of your creation
we might hear you declare once again
that everything is 'very good'.
Amen

Prayers for our care for others

83.

Game-changing God,
turn our 'we are weary' into 'we are ready';
turn our 'we are fearful' into 'we are faithful';
turn our cry for help into a call to hope.
Amen

Prayer is ultimately nothing to do with words, how long you spend on your knees, or even how you're feeling at the time. Prayer is simply being there for God with your hand up to volunteer, which is you saying, 'Here I am, use me.'
MARTYN PAYNE

Prayer is a deep conversation with God, beginning with communion and leading to transformation.
DANIEL WOLPERT

84.

Lord, your heartbeat for our world is love
and that love also holds all things together.
Take our small attempts at loving others
and weave them into your rescue plan
for the whole world,
as you work out Christ's down-to-earth love
in us and through us,
and grow your kingdom this day.
Amen

Over recent years I have become more and more aware that my relationship with God is not simply mediated through my mind and intellect but through every part of my body and each of my senses.
DAVID WALKER

85.

Creator God,
you have given us the gift of breath for our bodies
and the gift of prayer for our souls.
Likewise, may our active service of others
always go hand in hand with our faithful prayer
for them,
because it is both our working and our praying
that can transform the world.
Amen

The prayer 'your kingdom come' can be understood as a request for the Spirit to be at work for good, both in the lives of those who pray and in the whole world.
JOANNA COLLICUTT

Prayers for justice

86.

Peace-making God,
in Christ your love never ran out
when faced with hatred and ignorance,
cruelty and fear.
In our day, by the power of your cross,
bring together
fear-filled strangers
and prejudice-inspired enemies,
and break down the dividing walls between us.
Through your resurrection,
help us to breathe again
the compassionate and caring oxygen of Eden
by which we can recognise your likeness in every
human being,
rejoicing that you made each of us uniquely
different,
in the all-equal, all-welcome, all-people kingdom
of God.
Amen

87.

Forgive us, your people, O Lord,
because, again and again, we have
misunderstood your grace
misinterpreted your gospel
and misrepresented your glory,
and so have brought pain and shame
on our fellow human beings.
Forgive us for our history of violence
toward our neighbour, who is different,
and open our eyes instead
to the beauty of your likeness in every person,
without whom we cannot truly see Christ,
who is our only hope and our true salvation.
Amen

F.B. Meyer wrote, 'The greatest tragedy of life is not unanswered prayer, but unoffered prayer.'
MARK BRADFORD

We may not believe in God, but God never stops believing in us. In the same way God is always praying for us, even when we stop praying to God.
MARTYN PAYNE

Prayers for being disciples

88.

Holy and discipling God,
teach us through your Son,
who always did what he saw his Father doing.
Strengthen us by the Spirit,
who speaks to us of Jesus.
Guide us in the love of the Father,
who pours out his Spirit on us.
So that we may be your followers
all the days of our life.
Amen

As disciples, we are urged to seek the gifts of the Spirit and grow in the fruit of the Spirit. These all come from the Spirit of prayer who moves us from within to want these things.

MARTYN PAYNE

89.

Teach us, Father God,
how to listen to one another
so we might discover your wisdom;
how to lean on one another
so that we might model your love;
how to learn from one another
so that we might reflect your glory,
as co-disciples of Jesus
on our journey of faith.
Amen

Prayer is that inner dialogue with God which God is always initiating, because we have been created as spiritual beings in human bodies with a gravitational pull towards the One who is love.

MARTYN PAYNE

Prayer is key to understanding God's heart…
a God who is longing to welcome us 'home'.

JANE HOLLOWAY

Prayers for sharing the good news

90.

Lord Jesus, for whom
no one is last,
no one is lost,
no one is less,
give us a passion for all
who are still to come home to you,
that they might discover their true belonging
in the eternal company
of our welcoming, creator God.
Amen

91.

Father God,
help us to be witnesses to a fearful world
of your love that casts out fear
of your love that is as strong as death,
of your love that never ends,
because your banner over us is love.
Through Christ our Lord,
Amen

Named or unnamed, God is here.
Known or unknown, God is with us.
Recognised or unrecognised, God is present.
Loved or unloved, God is love.
God owes us nothing, yet chooses to give us everything.

MARTYN PAYNE

There is no magic formula that guarantees we get what we want in prayer... A mature understanding of prayer is a re-orientation towards praying according to God's will.

TONY HORSFALL

92.

Thank you, Father God, for your kingdom,
where everything is being turned the right way up:
where nobodies become somebodies,
where the overlooked are noticed,
where the marginalised take centre-stage
and where the forgotten are remembered.
Transform our lives in this upside-down world
through the power of the cross of Christ,
which turned defeat into victory,
suffering into glory
and an end into a new beginning.
Amen

The reason we pray isn't just to get God's help… we pray, because it gives God the chance to open our eyes – to remind us that we are not alone and to breathe new courage into us.

LYNDALL BYWATER

Do not practise long, drawn-out devotions, rather give yourself to prayer at intervals, as you would to food. Pious humbug is an invention of the devil.

THE RULE OF COMGALL

Prayers before we open up the Bible

93.

Thank you, Father God,
that your written word
leads us to Christ, your living Word,
and that through your Spirit
you promise to teach, challenge and inspire us
as we read our Bibles and spend time in prayer.
Rooted in your words and your presence,
and in fellowship with the Christian family
    around the world,
may we serve as your disciples in our day,
praying for God's kingdom to come,
and for people of all ages to grow into a
    living faith.
For your glory,
Amen

I've found a real liberty in drawing on the wealth and richness of prayers written by others and prayed through the centuries, which draw on scripture, particularly the book of Psalms.
MARK BRADFORD

94.

Lord God,
who have revealed your love through the stories of the Bible
help us to pass on its life-giving messages with sensitivity;
to handle its timeless truths with reverence;
to open up its deep treasures with skill
and to bring to life its powerful words with enthusiasm,
always trusting to the inspiration of your Holy Spirit.
In the name of Christ,
Amen

In the last book of the Bible, Christ describes himself as 'the Amen', which means Jesus is God's yes to our prayers, the one alongside us in our praying, and the one who assures us of God's blessing.
MARTYN PAYNE

95.

Lord, as we read the stories about you and words from you,
teach us something old and something new;
something for now and something for always;
something for me and something for others;
something known and something surprising;
something forgotten and something familiar;
something to grow your kingdom in us, in our community and in our world.
Amen

'For my thoughts are not your thoughts, neither are your ways my ways,' declares the Lord. 'As the heavens are higher than the earth, so are my ways higher than your ways and my thoughts than your thoughts.'
ISAIAH 55:8–9

Some prayers aren't answered because God himself is a greater answer than the thing we are asking for, and God wants to use our sense of need to draw us into a deeper relationship with himself.
PETE GREIG

Prayers about serving others

96.

Dear Lord,
strengthen us to serve you in response to
your love,
by giving freely to others without keeping a record
by working hard for others without counting
the cost
and by being a blessing to others without even
knowing it,
eager to do your will for your name's sake.
Amen

Prayer is a wonder, in every sense of the word. It is unfathomable and beautiful and joyfully real. The God we worship has always spoken, right from the very conception of creation, and God hasn't stopped.
LYNDALL BYWATER

Each day this week, let us begin our devotions, not with, 'Oh, good lord, it's morning,' but with 'Good morning, O Lord.'
MARTYN PAYNE

97.

Open-handed God,
you have blessed us in Christ
with every spiritual blessing in heaven;
help us to open our hearts and hands to others
so that the grace we have received
may inspire the generosity with which we give.
Amen

Come to prayer, conscious of the reverence God deserves, while asking God that everything in your day may more and more lead you to divine praise and service.

LARRY WARNER

Prayers on the theme of peace

98.

Lord Jesus,
you are the prince of peace;
you speak 'peace' to our hearts;
you are the peace that breaks down the dividing
    walls between us.
Help us to be your peacemakers
in this world of rivalries and fears,
so that your peace like a river
might flow freely and heal our land.
Amen

Writing Seven Sacred Spaces *and exploring the third chapter, 'Cell: being alone with God', underscored for me the oft-trumpeted truth that quality time with God is foundational to being a Christian.*
GEORGE LINGS

99.

God of all peace,
speak your peace to our restless souls,
bring your peace to our troubled lives,
establish your peace in our broken world,
because you have promised to mediate between
many nations
so that we should learn war no more.
Lord, work with us and in us towards that day.
Amen

In prayer, when words end in silence, we awaken to a new awareness and watchfulness. Silence shocks us out of numbness to the world and its needs; it sharpens our vision from its dullness of complacency and selfishness by focusing on the heart of all that matters.

DAVID COLE (BROTHER CASSIAN)

100.

Forgive us, Lord,
for turning caring for your world
into a competition as to who is the best,
and for pursuing that rivalry with a violence
that has broken your heart and damaged our
earthly home.
Refashion weaponry as wind turbines.
Repurpose bombs as bio-energy.
Recycle guns as green technology
as we seek peace and pursue it.
For your name's sake,
Amen

On earth prayer may often be unanswered, but it is definitely never unheard. And sometimes, beyond our understanding, God's best answer comes in heaven rather than on earth.

MARTYN PAYNE

Praying with the Bible

At that time people began to call on the name of the Lord.
GENESIS 4:26

The instinct to pray is part of how God has made us, and so the Bible records that from the very beginning people called upon the name of the Lord. Calling out to God does not need to involve a lot of words, and so, to complement the prayers in this collection, I am including here a list of 40 simple, intercessory prayers that can be found in the Bible. Each one has its own original author and context, but I believe we can also make these prayers our own; and because they are short, we can easily memorise them and thus take them with us throughout the day. You may recognise some of these, as they have become a regular part of the liturgy in some traditions of worship, and there are many examples from the Psalms. To use these prayers brings together two of the founding principles of BRF, namely that we should be earthed in scripture and rooted in prayer.

All the following verses are from the NRSV.

Let me take it upon myself to speak to the Lord, I who am but dust and ashes.

GENESIS 18:27

Here I am.

GENESIS 22:1

Not what I want but what you want.

MATTHEW 26:39

Search me, O God, and know my heart; test me and… see if there is any wicked way in me, and lead me in the way everlasting.

PSALM 139:23–24

I believe; help my unbelief!

MARK 9:24

Jesus, son of David, have mercy on me!

LUKE 18:38

My soul clings to you; your right hand upholds me.

PSALM 63:8

Here am I; send me.

ISAIAH 6:8

Speak, for your servant is listening.

1 SAMUEL 3:10

We do not know what to do, but our eyes are on you.

2 CHRONICLES 20:12

I will not let you go, unless you bless me.

GENESIS 32:26

Show me your glory.
EXODUS 33:18

Lord, if you choose, you can make me clean.
MATTHEW 8:2

Come, Lord Jesus!
REVELATION 22:20

Give your servant… an understanding mind… to discern between good and evil.
1 KINGS 3:9

Make me to know your ways, O Lord; teach me your paths.
PSALM 25:4

Into your hand I commit my spirit.
PSALM 31:5

The Lord watch between you and me, when we are absent one from the other.
GENESIS 31:49

O Lord, be gracious to us; we wait for you. Be our arm every morning, our salvation in the time of trouble.
ISAIAH 33:2

Heal me, O Lord, and I shall be healed; save me, and I shall be saved, for you are my praise.
JEREMIAH 17:14

For your name's sake, O Lord, pardon my guilt, for it is great.
PSALM 25:11

Be mindful of your mercy, O Lord, and of your steadfast love, for they have been from of old.
PSALM 25:6

You, O Lord, are a shield around me, my glory and the one who lifts up my head.
PSALM 3:3

Create in me a clean heart, O God, and put a new and right spirit within me.
PSALM 51:10

Your kingdom come.
LUKE 11:2

Give us each day our daily bread.
LUKE 11:3

Forgive us our sins.
LUKE 11:4

Do not bring us to the time of trial.
LUKE 11:4

Let the words of my mouth and the meditation of my heart be acceptable to you, O Lord.
PSALM 19:14

Teach me to do your will, for you are my God. Let your good spirit lead me on a level path.
PSALM 143:10

Let your ear be attentive and your eyes open to hear the prayer of your servant.
NEHEMIAH 1:6

O God, strengthen my hands.
NEHEMIAH 6:9

Guard me as the apple of the eye.
PSALM 17:8

Hear my prayer, O Lord; let my cry come to you.
PSALM 102:1

O Lord, open my lips, and my mouth will declare your praise.
PSALM 51:15

Lord, let me see again.
LUKE 18:41

Your face, Lord, do I seek.
PSALM 27:8

To you, O Lord, I lift up my soul.
PSALM 25:1

Hide me in the shadow of your wings.
PSALM 17:8

Teach me your way, O Lord, that I may walk in your truth; give me an undivided heart to revere your name.
PSALM 86:11

From the BRF archives: On prayer

From the *Brixton Parish Church Chronicle*, December 1921 (price 2p)

Written by Leslie G. Mannering, founder of BRF

Prayer and intercession are the supreme work of Christians. 'Work backed up by Prayer' is too often the practice, if not the ideal of the church. If the world is to be won, that order must be reversed and the Church learn to depend on 'Prayer backed up by Work'.

Those who desert their prayers in order to get more quickly to what they fondly call work, are like a stoker on a liner who puts out his furnace fires and tries to tow the ship himself.

We are so apt to be immersed in organisations, committees and plans, that we tend to become entangled in our own machinery… First and foremost there is prayer; not simply for ourselves but for the world in which we live.

The Fellowship of St Matthew [which became BRF] *will, I am convinced, become a mighty spiritual force… under the guidance of the Holy Spirit.*

Here are two BRF prayers quoted in the anniversary book produced for BRF's 80th birthday in 2002:

> We bless you, Lord,
> for all who teach us
> to love the scriptures
> and for all who help us
> to understand them;
> grant that
> in the written word
> we may encounter
> the living Word,
> your Son, our Saviour,
> Jesus Christ.
> Amen

> O God our Father,
> in the holy scriptures
> you have given us your word
> to be our teacher and guide:
> help us and all members of our fellowship
> to seek in our reading
> the guidance of the Holy Spirit
> that we may learn more of you
> and of your will for us,
> and so grow in likeness to your Son,
> Jesus Christ our Lord.
> Amen

Bibliography

Ian Adams, quoted in Andrew Roberts (ed.), *Holy Habits Bible Reflections: Prayer: 40 readings and reflections* (BRF, 2019).

Timothy Bavin OSB, quoted in Richard Frost, *Life with St Benedict* (BRF, 2019).

Mark Bradford, *The Space Between: The disruptive seasons we want to hide from, and why we need them* (BRF, 2021).

Lyndall Bywater, *Prayer in the Making: Trying it, talking it, sustaining it* (BRF, 2019).

Lyndall Bywater, quoted in Andrew Roberts (ed.), *Holy Habits Bible Reflections: Prayer: 40 readings and reflections* (BRF, 2019).

Joan Chittister, quoted in George Lings, *Seven Sacred Spaces: Portals to deeper community life in Christ* (BRF, 2020).

David Cole, *The Art of Peace: Life lessons from Christian mystics* (BRF, 2021).

Joanna Collicutt, *When You Pray: Daily Bible reflections on the Lord's Prayer* (BRF, 2019).

Stephen Cottrell, *Come and See: Learning from the life of Peter* (BRF, 2020).

Gordon Giles, *At Home in Lent: An exploration of Lent through 46 objects* (BRF, 2018).

Peter Greig, quoted in Jane Holloway, *Prayer: A beginner's guide* (BRF, 2009).

Jane Holloway, *Prayer: A beginner's guide* (BRF, 2009).

Tony Horsfall, *Mentoring Conversations: 30 key topics to explore together* (BRF, 2020).

Father Mychal Judge, chaplain to the New York Fire Brigade, quoted in Helen Julian, *Franciscan Footprints: Following Christ in the ways of Francis and Clare* (BRF, 2020).

C.S. Lewis, quoted in Sally Welch, *Journey to Contentment: Pilgrimage principles for everyday life* (BRF, 2020).

Martin Luther, quoted in Sally Welch, *Journey to Contentment: Pilgrimage principles for everyday life* (BRF, 2020).

Michael Mitton, quoted in Andrew Roberts (ed.), *Holy Habits Bible Reflections: Prayer: 40 readings and reflections* (BRF, 2019).

Lucy Moore, *Family Prayer Time: On the journey together* (BRF, 2018).

Ann Persson, *The Circle of Love: Praying with Rublev's icon of the Trinity* (BRF, 2010).

Andrew Roberts (ed.), *Holy Habits Bible Reflections: Prayer: 40 readings and reflections* (BRF, 2019).

Larry Warner, *Discovering the Spiritual Exercises of Saint Ignatius* (BRF, 2020).

Sally Welch, *Journey to Contentment: Pilgrimage principles for everyday life* (BRF, 2020).

Daniel Wolpert, *Creating a life with God: The call of ancient prayer practices* (Upper Rooms Books, 2003).

Index of Bible references

Prayer and BRF

First and foremost, prayer

BRF's founder, Revd Leslie Mannering, sought to galvanise the spiritual lives of his south-London congregation through prayer, Bible reading and fellowship. He wrote in his church newsletter in November 2021:

'I believe… we all need to get back, absolutely back, to the fundamentals of our faith.

'First and foremost there is prayer,' he went on, 'not simply for ourselves, but for the world in which we live. How can St Matthew's be a mighty spiritual force in Brixton? Only in one way: only if our congregation as a solid whole realises that prayer and intercession is their supreme work as Christians.'

From the outset, his duplicated Bible reading notes included prayers for local, national and international needs – prayers for provision and for peace, for wisdom, resilience and hope – timeless, universal prayers as urgent today as they were 100 years ago.

But Leslie Mannering had a deep and distinctive understanding of the true power and place of prayer. He wrote:

'Work backed up by prayer is too often the practice, if not the ideal, of the church. If the world is to be won, that order must be reversed and the church learn to depend on prayer backed up by work… When, in any parish, there is a large body of people who really pray and really intercede, there are literally no limits to the possibilities of spiritual advance.'

This is precisely the vision of prayer that BRF seeks to embody today, honouring our founder's vision and recognising his wisdom. We long always to be an organisation in which prayer is backed up by our work, and not the other way round. This frees the Spirit to blow where it will, leading us into new adventures, helping us to discern God's calling, rather than making our plans and seeking a rubber-stamp of divine approval.

Prayer infuses the life of BRF. From our daily staff prayers, our weekly prayer email from Chief Executive Richard Fisher, our printed prayer diary produced three times a year and the prayers that conclude every one of our Bible reading notes, to our annual Festival of Prayer, and the intersecting networks of faithful pray-ers without whom our different ministries could not function let alone thrive, prayer continues to be a constant, formative strand in the DNA of BRF.

Championed by our Prayer Advocate, Martyn Payne, who has written this moving and wide-ranging collection of prayers for personal and corporate use, prayer has always been and will always be the oxygen of the organisation. It is no accident that alongside this volume, another of our special 'Centenary Classics' is a commemorative edition of *The Jesus Prayer* by Simon Barrington-Ward, first published in 1996.

In its simplest form, the Jesus Prayer consists of ten words, 'Lord Jesus Christ, Son of God, have mercy on me.' Originating with the Desert Fathers and Mothers, the prayer embraces adoration, praise and joy as well as confession, surrender and yearning for wholeness. Slow, rhythmic repetition takes the pray-er deep into the heart of God. The prayer is loved and practised across the world.

In his introduction to the 2007 edition of *The Jesus Prayer*, Simon Barrington-Ward wrote:

'I hope the book will help many, many more Christians throughout a wide variety of churches and fellowships to be drawn into stillness, and in that stillness… to be drawn into a deeper communion with God, in Christ, through the Spirit. I hope it will lead a large number of new readers to the secret of unceasing prayer, to a whole way of praying that continues day and night, while we are working, eating, meeting with each other and even while we sleep.'

To which BRF says, Amen.

> Continue steadfastly in prayer, being watchful in it with thanksgiving.
> COLOSSIANS 4:2 (ESV)

Eley McAinsh
Press and Media Officer

Friends of BRF

I never fail to be amazed by the generosity of our supporters.

BRF is a remarkable charity, but we can only do what we do with the help of our faithful supporters: volunteers, people who pray for us and spread the word about our work, and people who support us financially, both individuals who give donations and legacies, and charitable trusts.

Many of our supporters have become 'Friends of BRF', choosing to make a regular monthly gift to help ensure that our work can be sustained and developed in the coming years. Every single donation, whether occasional or regular, small or large, makes a huge difference and I, along with all my colleagues here at BRF, thank God for each one.

If you'd like to help support Living Faith and our wider ministry, please visit **brf.org.uk/give**, contact a member of the fundraising team by email at **giving@brf.org.uk** or call **01235 462305** to speak to one of us direct.

With heartfelt thanks

Julie

Julie MacNaughton,
Head of Fundraising MCIOF(Dip)

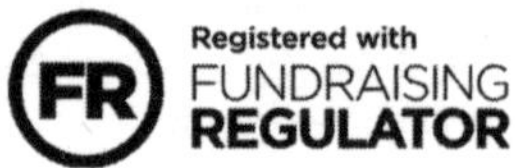

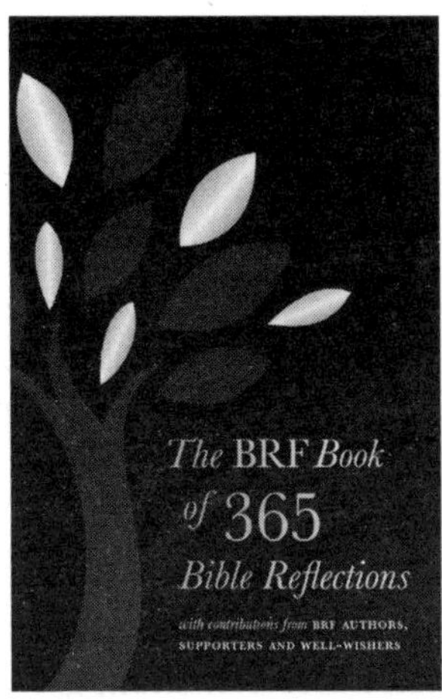

The Bible is at the heart of BRF's work, and this special anniversary collection is a celebration of the Bible for BRF's centenary year.

Bringing together a fantastically wide-ranging writing team of authors, supporters and well-wishers from all areas of BRF's work, this resource is designed to help us go deeper into the story of the Bible and reflect on how we can share it in our everyday lives.

Including sections which lead us through the Bible narrative as well as thematic and seasonal sections, it is the perfect daily companion to resource your spiritual journey.

The BRF Book of 365 Bible Reflections

With contributions from BRF authors, supporters and well-wishers

Edited by Karen Laister and Olivia Warburton

978 1 80039 100 0, 416 pages £14.99 (hardback)

brfonline.org.uk

SIMON BARRINGTON WARD
The Jesus Prayer
BRF CENTENARY CLASSICS

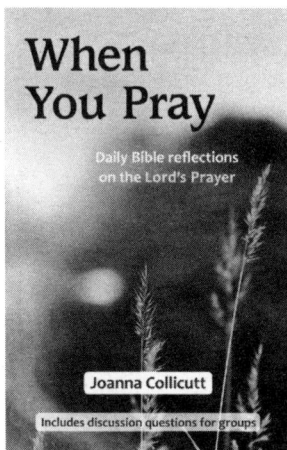

Daily inspiration

Bible reading notes to sustain, comfort, inform and challenge

If you have enjoyed these prayers, you might like to continue your walk with God with the help of our popular Bible reading notes. There are five series to choose from, each with a different style and focus, but all designed to encourage daily Bible reading, reflection and prayer. There's almost certainly one that's perfect for you.

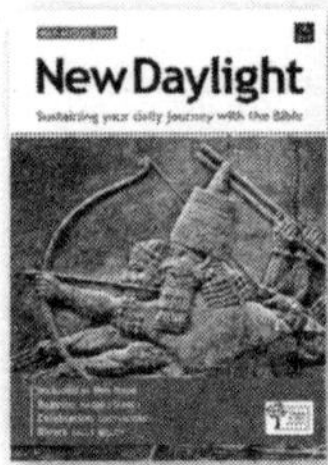

New Daylight
Our most popular series, *New Daylight*, is for everyone on their daily walk with God. Enjoy getting to know the writers, from well-loved regulars to exciting new voices. *New Daylight* has everything you need in one pocket-sized volume, including full Bible reading, reflection and prayer. There's also a large-format deluxe edition.

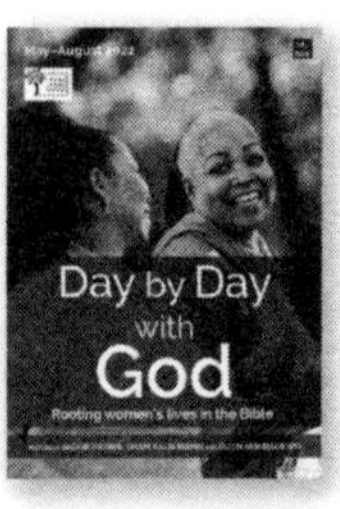

Day by Day with God
This series is specifically written for women, to help readers root their lives ever more firmly in the Bible. All the contributors are women and write from a woman's perspective. Whatever your current situation in life, you will be inspired and encouraged by these notes.

For more information on all our Bible reading notes, go to **brfonline.org.uk/our-notes**

Bible Reflections for Older People
These notes grew out of our Anna Chaplaincy ministry and are written by older people, for older people. Each issue contains 40 undated reflections, written to bring comfort and encouragement, and a magazine section containing interviews, features, poems and a welcome letter from Anna Chaplaincy founder and pioneer, Debbie Thrower.

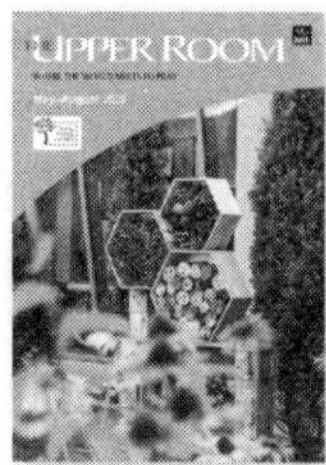

The Upper Room
'Where the world meets to pray' is a lovely description of *The Upper Room*. Uniquely, the readers of this series are also the writers, with contributions gathered from around the world. It has a worldwide readership of some three million, with over 70 different editions in 40 languages, and BRF is privileged to publish the UK edition.

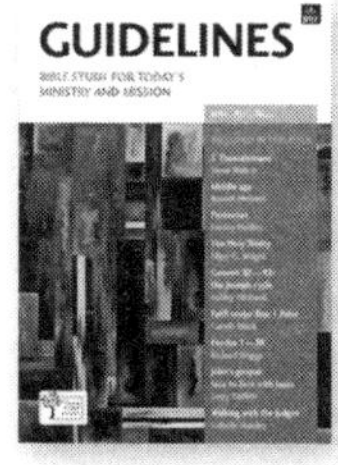

Guidelines
Guidelines is our most serious and theological series and is popular amongst ministers, leaders and students. Each issue offers four months of in-depth Bible study written by leading scholars. Contributors are drawn from around the world, as well as the UK, and represent a stimulating and thought-provoking breadth of Christian tradition.

Bible reading apps
For readers on the move, we have iOS and Android app editions of *Guidelines*, *New Daylight* and *Day by Day with God*.